# FENCING
## is for me

# FENCING
## is for me

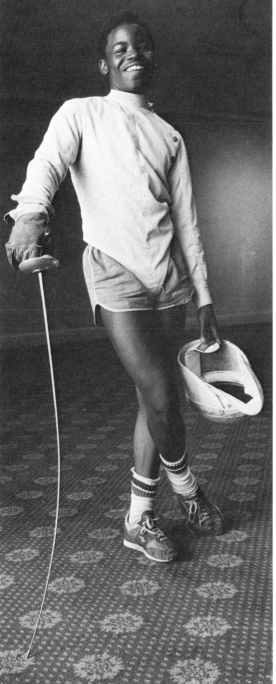

Art Thomas

photographs by
Julia Sheehan-Burke

Lerner Publications Company    Minneapolis

The author and photographer would like to thank Bill Reith and the members of the Alcazar Fencing Club, Cleveland Heights, Ohio. Special thanks also go to the main characters in the book, including Kevin Hunter, Wilbur Wheeler, and Peter Ciemins.

**Editorial Consultant: Robert van der Wege**
**Coach, Minnesota Excalibur**

LIBRARY OF CONGRESS CATALOGING IN PUBLICATION DATA

**Thomas, Art, 1952-**
   Fencing is for me.

   (The Sports for me books)
   Summary: Text and photographs follow Kevin as he learns the techniques of fencing.
   1. Fencing—Juvenile literature. [1. Fencing]
I. Sheehan-Burke, Julia, ill.  II. Title.
III. Series.
GV1147.T49          796.8'6          81-20716
   ISBN 0-8225-1129-0          AACR2

Manufactured in the United States of America

International Standard Book Number: 0-8225-1129-0
Library of Congress Catalog Card Number: 81-20716

2   3   4   5   6   7   8   9   10   90   89   88   87   86   85   84   83

Hello! My name is Kevin. I've just finished competing in my first fencing tournament. Fencing is an ancient sport involving the use of pointed weapons. Before I started fencing, I thought that it would be like the sword fighting I saw in movies. But since then I've learned that fencing has changed.

Fencing is not used for fights and battles anymore. It is now a sport with special rules and equipment. Fencing is hard work, but it's a lot of fun, too. I'd like to tell you about how I started fencing.

One day there was a play at school. Two of the actors had to **duel**, or settle an argument by fighting with swords. To win the argument, one of them had to win the sword fight. The duel on stage was very exciting. I wanted to learn how to use a sword like that. So my teacher introduced me to Bill, the man who had taught the actors how to fence.

Bill taught fencing classes. He told me that I was old enough to study the sport. But in order to join his class, I would need my parents' permission and a note from my doctor saying I was healthy. My parents said that I could study fencing if I would be willing to practice. I had no trouble passing the doctor's physical exam, so I was ready to begin.

At my first class, Bill showed me the fencing **weapons**. Fencers don't call the weapons swords. There are three kinds of fencing weapons: the **épée** (ay-PAY), the **foil**, and the **saber**. There are different rules used for each weapon. Bill said that I would begin with foil fencing.

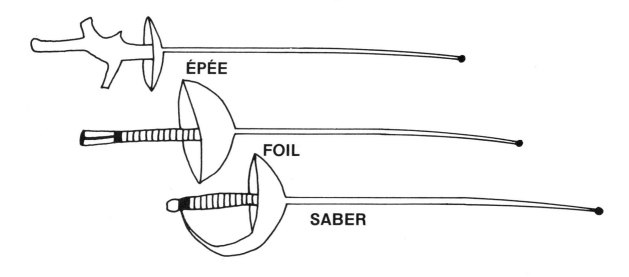

The foil is a **point** weapon. This means that only the point, or tip, can be used to score **touches**, which are also called **hits**. The épée is also a point weapon. In saber fencing, however, you can score hits with parts of the blade edge as well as with the point.

The foil has a long, thin blade that bends when it touches an opponent. I was glad to find out that the point is covered by a rubber tip so it cannot pierce your skin. You hold the foil on the **grip**. Your hand will be protected by a wide piece of metal called a **guard**.

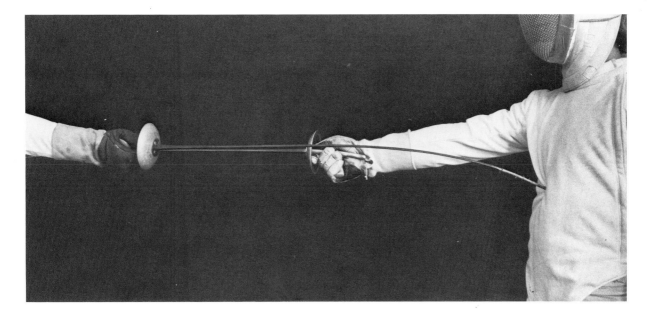

Bill explained that the object of fencing is to touch your opponent with your weapon and to prevent your opponent's blade from landing on you. Hits that land on a special **target area** are scored as touches. In foil fencing, the target area is the torso.

If you hit your opponent off the target area, no touch is scored. But the match stops for a moment so the fencers can return to the ready position. Each valid touch is worth one point. The first fencer to score five touches against his or her opponent is the winner of the **bout**, or match.

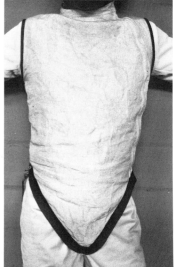

Before I could begin working with the foil, I had to put on the proper clothing. Fencers dress in white. They wear heavy jackets and padded white pants, and they wear a glove on their **foil hand**.

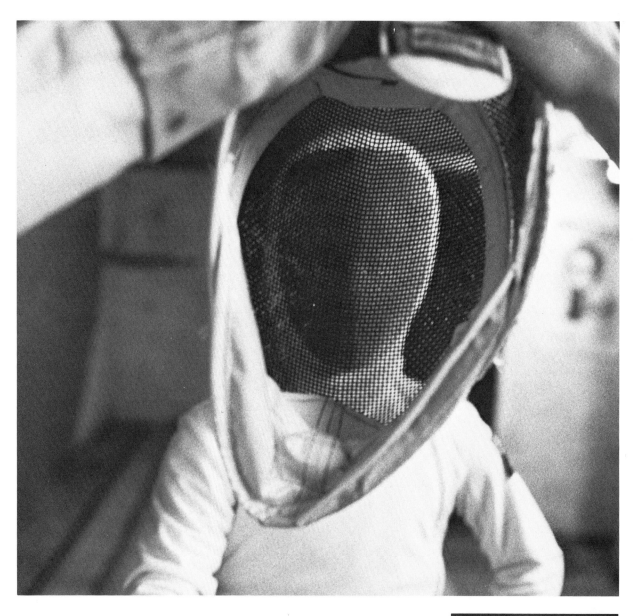

One of the most important pieces of equipment is the **mask**. On the front of the mask is a stiff wire screen. The screen protects your face and ears, but you can still see out. A **bib**, which covers your neck, is attached to the mask. The first time I tried on all of the equipment, I felt funny. But I knew I'd get used to it.

Next Bill showed me how to hold the foil. Your last three fingers should go on the longer side of the grip. A little higher on the grip, place your index finger against the guard. Your thumb should be flat on top of the grip.

Bill said that holding the foil this way would give me good control. Many fencing skills depend on small movements of the fingers only, so control is important. He told me to hold the foil firmly, but not too tightly, or my arm would get tired quickly.

Next I learned the **salute**. The salute is the polite greeting that begins every bout. The salute is performed from a position of attention. Your front foot should point toward your opponent. Hold your heels together and point your rear foot to the side. Hold your mask with your free arm.

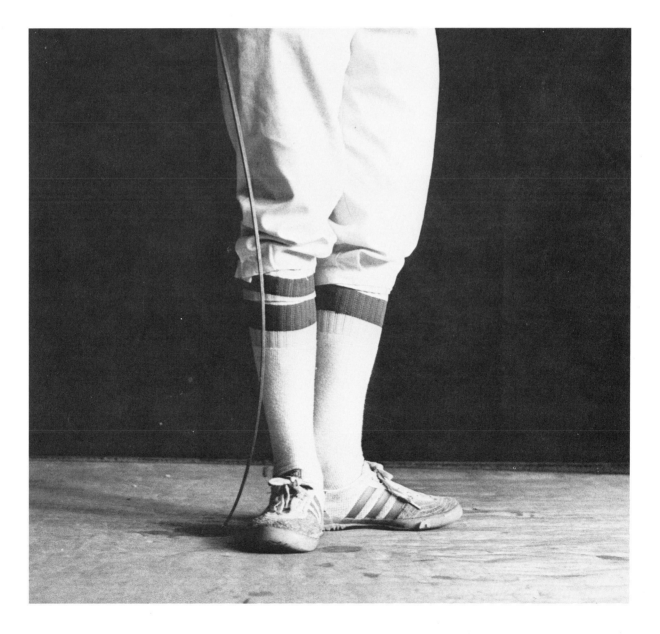

There are three parts to the simple salute.
First point your foil toward the floor,
holding your arm straight. Next point
the blade toward your opponent at about
shoulder height. Finally the foil is pointed
upward. Bring the guard close to your chin.
The back of your hand will be facing your
opponent.

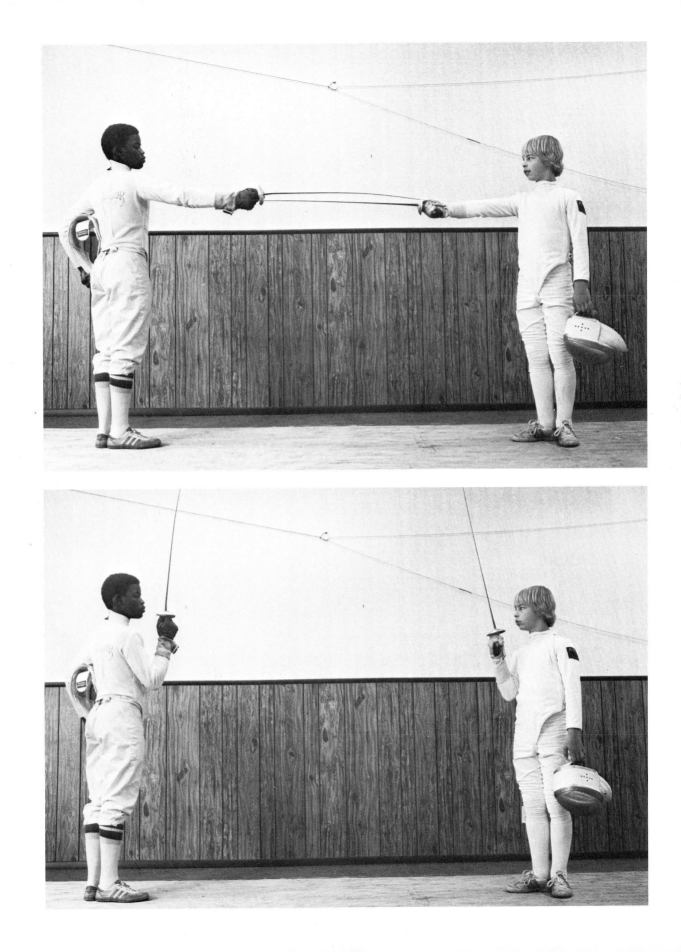

After the salute is completed, put on the mask with your free hand. Then move into the **on-guard** position. For this position, step forward with your front foot until both feet are apart at about shoulder width. Then bend your knees and center your weight between your feet. Your foil arm should hold the weapon with the tip at your opponent's chin level.

The palm should be up, and the elbow should be bent. Hold your free arm up and out of the way behind your head. Pulling the arm back like this will make a smaller target area for your opponent.

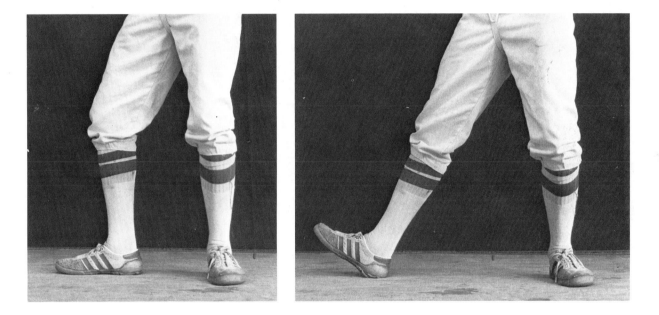

The basic footwork is done from the on-guard position. Moving forward is called **advancing**. You advance by moving your front foot forward. Land on the heel of the foot and roll forward to your toe. Then move your rear foot forward the same distance.

Moving backward is called **retreating**. The rear foot moves first, and the front foot follows. Retreating can take you out of the attacking range of your opponent. But your retreat is limited by a boundary. The boundary forms a field of play called the **strip**.

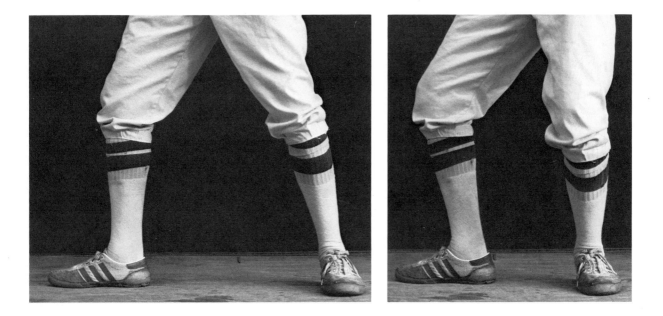

The strip is 2 meters (6 feet, 7 inches) wide and 14 meters (46 feet) long. The first time you cross the end boundary with both feet, you are given a warning. But the second time you cross this line, your opponent is awarded a touch against you.

I practiced advancing and retreating with Peter. Peter was about my size, and he had been fencing for over a year. Bill watched us practice and corrected my mistakes. Sometimes I forgot to keep my free arm pulled back, and Bill had to remind me. Bill also made sure that I didn't drag my feet or move my head up and down when I advanced. Bill said that if I watched Peter's movements and moved level with his shoulder, then I would be advancing correctly.

As I became more comfortable with the fencing equipment, I began to learn some basic attacking moves. The attacker is the first person to straighten his or her foil arm and to move toward the target. This person remains the attacker until he or she touches the target or until the opponent has defended himself or herself against the attack.

I then learned the **lunge**. The lunge is a sudden attack on the opponent. The back leg provides the power for this move. To do the lunge, point your foil straight toward your target. Lift your front leg and extend your back leg with a powerful thrust. At the same time, bring your free arm straight down. The rear arm will help you balance.

**LUNGE**

To recover from the lunge, push your weight back off of the front leg. Another way to recover is to bring your rear foot forward. Either way, you will return to the on-guard position. During the recovery, make sure that your arm is still extended for protection.

If your opponent assumes the attacking position first, you will have to defend yourself before you can return the attack. One defensive move is the **parry**. When you parry, you use your foil to **deflect**, or turn away, your opponent's blade. You should use the strong part of your blade, near the guard, against your opponent's weaker tip.

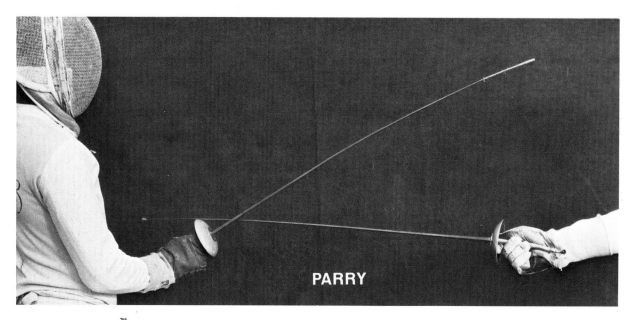

PARRY

Whenever foil blades are crossed, we say that they are **engaged**. Engagements are sometimes identified by the target area where the engagement occurs. The target area is divided into four parts by imaginary lines.

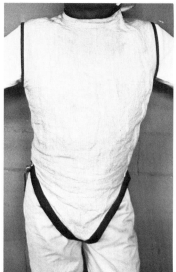

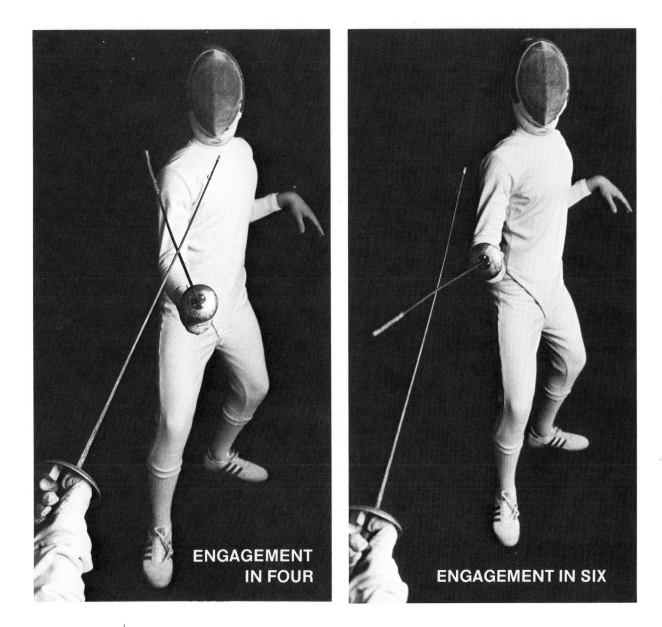

**ENGAGEMENT IN FOUR**

**ENGAGEMENT IN SIX**

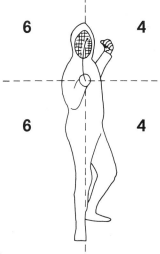

The top two parts are named by the numbers four and six. When your opponent's blade is to the left of your blade, we call this an **engagement in four**. When your opponent's blade is to the right side of your blade, we call this an **engagement in six**. There are other engagements in the lower parts of the target. Bill said I would learn about them later.

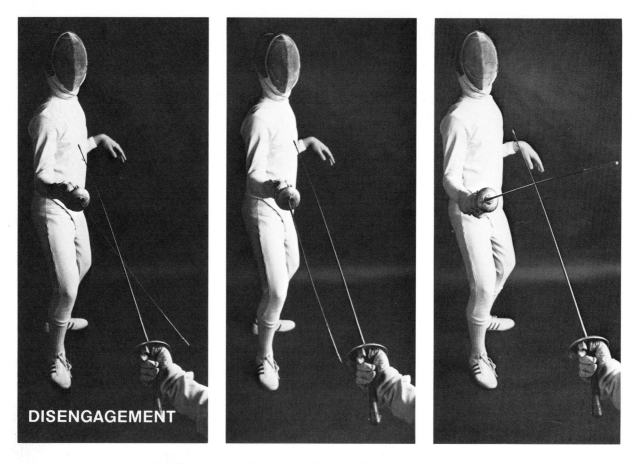

**DISENGAGEMENT**

A fencer whose blade is engaged may change his engagement from four to six or from six to four. To do this, first you separate the blades. Then you dip the blade point under your opponent's blade, bringing your blade up to the other side of his or her foil. This dipping movement is called a **disengagement**. Disengagements should be done with finger action only. Your arm and hand should not move. Remember to raise the point to your opponent's chin level after you've completed the move.

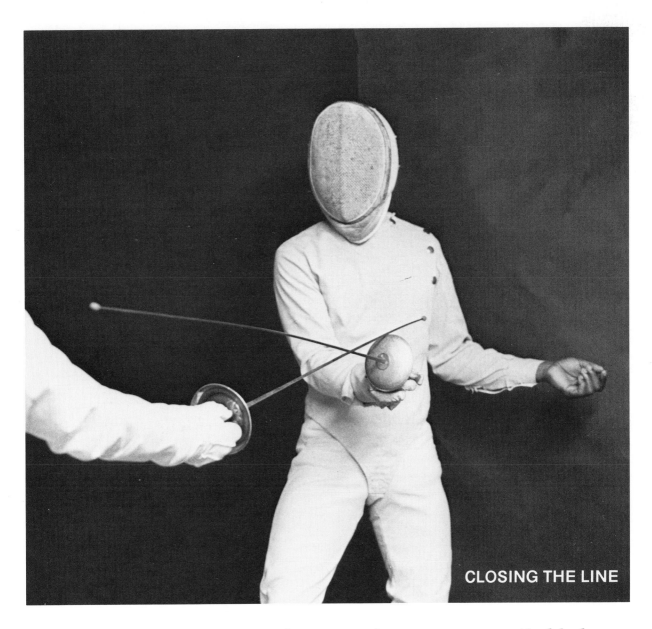

**CLOSING THE LINE**

In order to push your opponent's blade to the outside, away from your body, you may want to engage blades. To do this, place your guard directly in front of your opponent's point of attack. The guard will keep the point away and prevent a touch. This blocking action is called **closing the line**.

**RIPOSTE**

One follow-up move to a successful defense is the **riposte** (rih-POST). The riposte is a quick return attack that is done in a continuous motion after a parry. Move in before your opponent has recovered from the attack. Then simply extend your point and arm and touch your target.

If your opponent has already returned to the on-guard position, you may have to follow your arm extension with a lunge.

I got really tired from practicing all these fencing skills. My mind was tired from concentrating, and my body was tired from the exercise. But Bill said that in order to improve, I would have to practice and condition my body.

Everyone at the club warms up before practicing. Fencers must do exercises every day at home, too. Muscles should be stretched by steady pressure, not by bouncing. We do leg stretches by sitting with our feet spread apart. Then we lean over each leg for about 15 seconds. Next we extend our bodies straight forward.

We do two standing stretches, the side stretch and the lunge stretch. The side stretch is done by leaning over one leg, holding it, and then leaning to the other side. The lunge stretch is done by extending one leg forward and stretching it.

Another important part of training is running. Running helps keep me in shape so I won't get tired easily. I try to run every day.

I also use weight-lifting equipment to help build strength in my arms and legs. I especially need to strengthen my foil arm so that I can hold the foil longer without getting tired. Weight lifting is hard work, but I can feel myself getting stronger.

Every beginning fencer has trouble keeping his or her balance. To improve my balance, I practice on a bongo board. You try to center your weight over the tube that supports the board. I like practicing on the bongo board, and it's really helping my balancing skills.

After several months of training and practicing fencing skills, Bill told me there was going to be a tournament in our town. Even beginners could enter! So I began to practice every spare minute. I usually practiced at the club with a partner. But at home I practiced in front of a mirror. I also used target dummies to improve my accuracy.

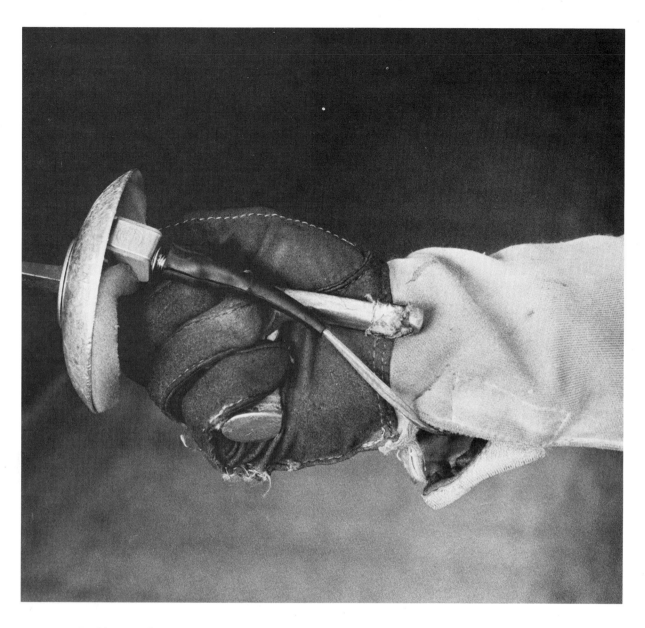

Bill said that the tournament would be scored electronically. When fencing is scored electronically, the jacket has a fine wire screen in parts of it. The foil is also wired. So when the point lands on the screen, a light flashes and a buzzer sounds. This tells the director in charge of the bout that there has been a touch. An electric cord attaches to the back of the foil with a plug.

The long cord is kept on a spool at the end of the strip so that you don't trip during a bout. Sometimes I wore the electronic equipment when I practiced so that I could get used to it.

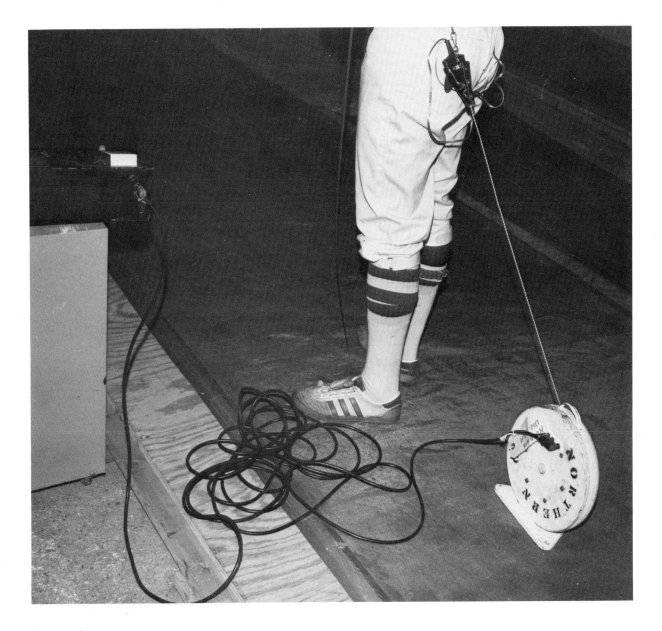

I was worried about getting an electric
shock, but Bill said that wouldn't happen.
I learned to forget about the wires and
cords and to concentrate on my attack
instead. If I took my mind off the bout,
my opponent could score. I'd get angry
at myself if that happened.

When the day of the tournament finally arrived, I was so excited! I got to the tournament early. I found out that I would be fencing in a junior division for fencers under the age of 16. There were 20 fencers in my division. Some of the boys and girls were as young as 9 or 10 years old.

The director of the tournament explained how the winner would be determined. He split the people in our division into three smaller groups, or **pools**. We would each fence everyone else in our pool. The best three fencers from each pool would then compete again. The director called this a **round robin**.

The director started and stopped each bout. His decisions in scoring were final. I was nervous during my first bout against Tom, and I lost. My second bout was against a girl named Karen. She was very good, and I lost again.

I was really determined to concentrate the third time I fenced. I was careful, and I was able to parry and riposte to my opponent's attacks. We both scored several times, and I was leading, 4 to 3.

My opponent took the offensive as the bout went on. I retreated out of attack range, but I was getting close to the end line. I knew I couldn't retreat any further without stepping over the line. So I timed my move carefully and parried my opponent's lunge.

Now I took the attacking position. I moved in fast before my opponent could fully recover from his lunge. I scored again, and I won my first bout!

I did my best against the rest of the fencers in my pool. But many of them were better than I was. When my friend Wilbur beat me, I didn't advance to the second round.

I wasn't too disappointed, though. I had made a lot of friends, and I knew that I would see them again in other tournaments. I'll keep fencing, because I know that there are many skills I still have to learn. Besides, I really love the sport. I know that fencing is for me!

# Words about FENCING

**ADVANCE:** To move forward on the strip

**ATTACK:** Any offensive move that threatens the target

**BOUT:** A fencing match

**CHANGING ENGAGEMENT:** Switching the side of your foil making contact with your opponent's blade

**CLOSING THE LINE:** Putting your guard in front of your opponent's point of attack, enabling you to push the blade to the outside

**DISENGAGEMENT:** The dipping motion made with the blade, bringing it around to the other side of the opponent's blade

**DUEL:** An old-fashioned way of settling disputes by fighting with swords

**ENGAGEMENT:** When two blades are in contact

**FEINT:** To provoke a parry by a mock attack toward one area of the target with the intention of hitting another area

**FOIL:** A point weapon used in fencing

**GUARD:** The part of the foil that separates the blade from the handle

**LUNGE:** An attacking move in which the attacker's body and weapon arm are moving forward toward the opponent

**ON GUARD:** The ready position in fencing

**PARRY:** A move that forces your opponent's tip away from your target area

**POOL:** A small group of fencers competing against each other in a tournament

**RETREAT:** To move backward on the strip

**RIPOSTE:** An attack made by a fencer who has just successfully defended an attack from the opponent

**SALUTE:** The formal greeting fencers perform at the start of a bout

**STRIP:** The field of play for a fencing bout

**TARGET AREA:** The area of a fencer's body that may be touched to score a valid hit

**TOUCH:** Reaching the target area with the tip of the foil blade moving slightly forward. Each valid touch is worth one point.

**TOUCHÉ (too-SHAY):** A French word meaning "touched"

**WEAPONS:** The foils, épées, and sabers used in fencing

## ABOUT THE AUTHOR:

ART THOMAS is active in sports as an instructor, a participant, and a fan. As a drama and composition teacher in Cleveland, Ohio, Mr. Thomas is also involved with professional and community theater, both as an actor and a director. In addition, he writes travel and feature articles for newspapers and magazines and has authored other books in the *Sports for Me* series.

## ABOUT THE PHOTOGRAPHER

JULIA SHEEHAN-BURKE is an ardent fencer and loves the sport as much as she loves her camera. A photography instructor and freelance photographer/artist, Ms. Sheehan-Burke's work has focused on education and the development of children. She has written articles for several educational journals and magazines.